D1751370

GOODBYE HYPERVIGILANCE

Copyright © 2021 My Adoptee Truth.
Author - Lora K. Joy
Front cover illustration and internal illustrations by Laura Foote.

All rights reserved. No part of this publication may be reproduced, distributed, or transmitted in any form or by any means, including photocopying, recording, or other electronic or mechanical methods, without the prior written permission of the publisher, except in the case of brief quotations embodied in critical reviews and certain other noncommercial uses permitted by copyright law.

ISBN: 978-1-7369900-1-8 (Paperback)
ISBN: 978-1-7369900-0-1 (Hardcover)

Any references to historical events, real people, or real places are used fictitiously. Names, characters, and places are products of the author's imagination.

Front cover illustration and internal illustrations by Laura Foote.

Printed by Ingram Spark, in the United States of America.

First printing edition 2021.

Publisher: My Adoptee Truth

THIS IS SARAH.
Sarah was adopted when she was a baby. See how calm Sarah looks: but she isn't!

Sarah is hyperviligilant. Other just can't see it.
Being hypervigilant means you're on alert and sensitive to your surroundings. She thinks it is her personality, how she's wired, who she really is.

But it isn't.

When babies are born and get separated from their moms, they get scared...

.....and stay that way for a long time.

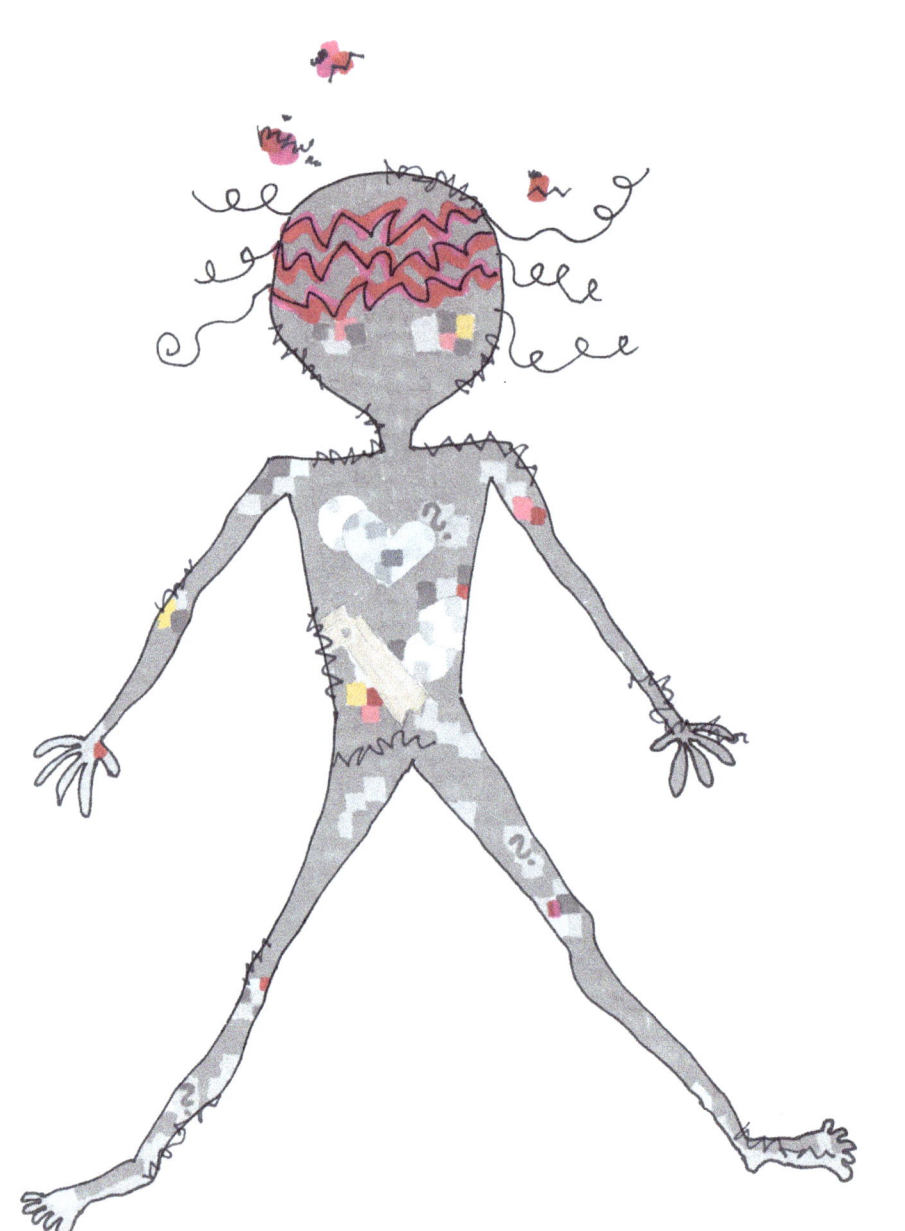

Everyone's brains are wired to look for danger, but adoptees are also looking for the same danger like being taken from their mother.

Because of this, adoptees do not have a foundation of feeling safe like non adopted people.

No matter the situation,
Sarah can look calm on the outside...

and be hypervigilant
on the inside.

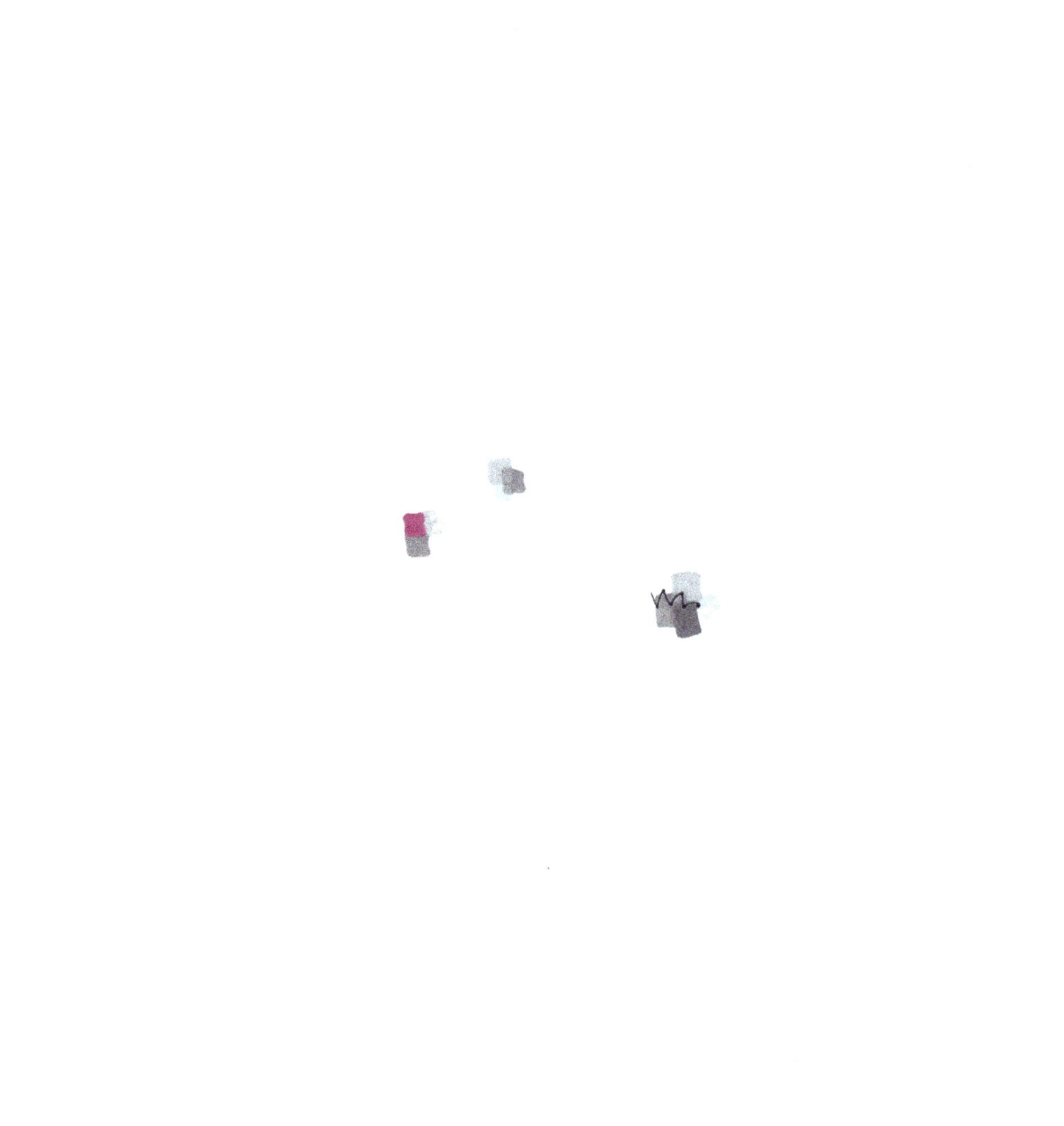

Looking for danger, makes Sarah's nerves tense.

When Sarah grew up and knew she could take care of herself, she was no longer in danger, but the hyperviliance did not go away.

It was always with her, like a steady hum in her brain. She was on the lookout for emotional danger—looking calm on the outside, but hypervigilant on the inside.

Sarah thought this hypervigilance was a part of who she was. She thought worrying helped protect her from bad things happening.

Sarah talked to her therapist about this worry to control things.

"Is this just a part of who I am?"

"I wonder if this being on high alert might be an old coping mechanism, your body remembers how dangerous it felt when you were separated from your biological mom."

Maybe this coping skill does not serve you anymore. You are competent and capable and if something bad happens, you will handle it."

"Really?! you mean I dont have to be on high alert all the time?"

"You're right, I can handle situations when they arise."

What happened next felt like a miracle.

Sarah's body received the message
of her therapist's words; it was not a decision but her body
and mind relaxed.

After 40 years of living with tight nerves and a hum in her brain, Sarah's nervous system relaxed, her shoulders dropped and the hum went away.

It was such a relief, but it also felt like Sarah had lost something. Adoption had put her on high alert from day one and hypervigilance had seeped into all corners of her life.

She was so used to her "friend" hypervigilance being with her.

She kept looking for it. She peeped around corners thinking it was going to jump out and latch on to her again.

But it didn't. She wondered if ths was how non adopted people felt all the time.

Sarah knows that at some point there will be legitimate things to cause anxiety in her life, but she is not going to worry about them until they happen. Sarah is now going to live in the moment and experience life with new eyes.

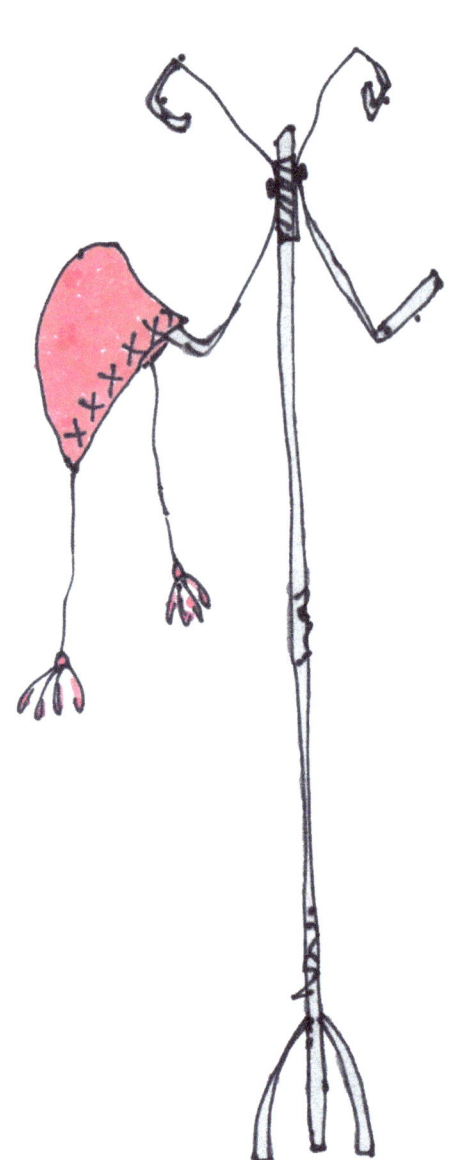

Goodbye hypervigilance,
you are not welcome here anymore!

"Thank you Anne, Lesli, Libby and Jon for your encouragement and support on this project. Thank you, Laura, for your perfect drawings and Carrie for bringing the hat to life!"

CPSIA information can be obtained
at www.ICGtesting.com
Printed in the USA
LVHW061759030621
689284LV00003B/124